GUARDIANS

Peter Morris
GUARDIANS

OBERON BOOKS
LONDON

www.oberonbooks.com

First published in 2005 by Oberon Books Ltd
521 Caledonian Road, London N7 9RH
Tel: 020 7607 3637 / Fax: 020 7607 3629
e-mail: info@oberonbooks.com
www.oberonbooks.com

A catalogue record for this book is available from the British
Library.

ISBN: 978-1-84002-642-9

Cover design by Dan Steward / Oberon Books

Printed and bound in Great Britain
by Marston Book Services Limited, Didcot.

To Joseph,
who knows that nothing's black and white
except penguins, pandas, and newspapers,

and to Muffy and Marian,
who made it all possible
and may possibly
regret it all now.

This conscience could be allayed only by taking upon itself the pain, the misery, the dinginess, and the pathetic but hard vulgarities of a stale and hopeless period... His masochism, indeed, extended to culture... One can see that deadly pain, which had long been his subject, had seized him completely and obliged him to project a nightmare, as Wells had done in his last days, upon the future.

– V S Pritchett, *George Orwell: An Obituary* (1950)

Without love, ladies and gentlemen...there is only rape.

– Kiki DuRane

Characters

The English Boy
is handsome. He is in his 20s, and wears the uniform
of a London tabloid journalist (dark pinstripe
suit, sober tie with Windsor knot.) Although his
job requires him to adopt an unconvincing South
London accent at times, beneath it we hear his
real voice: that of the Oxbridge elite. He speaks
accordingly, deadpan mixed with deadly panache.

The American Girl
is plain. She is in her 20s, and wears the uniform
of an American military prisoner (orange jumpsuit,
shoes without laces.) Although her job required her
to adopt an unconvincing Standard American accent
at times, beneath it we hear her real voice: that of
West Virginia's rural poor. She speaks accordingly,
despair mixed with defiance.

Guardians is set in the present,
and is performed without interval.

Guardians premiered in August 2005 on the Edinburgh Fringe, and received a 2005 Fringe First Award. The play was staged at the Pleasance Cavern by the Mahwaff Theatre Company (Katrin McMillan, producer) with the following cast:

ENGLISH BOY, Hywel John
AMERICAN GIRL, MyAnna Buring

Director Michael Longhurst
Designer Mike Britton

Author's Note

The English Boy and the American Girl in this play are fictional, and *Guardians* is a work of fiction. For those who prefer fact, I can recommend two books. Mark Danner's excellent study *Torture and Truth* offers glimpses, within its many pages, of a similar American girl. And *The Insider* by Piers Morgan tells a story, in its first few pages, that suggests a similar English boy. Danner's book is full of scrupulous factual detail. Morgan's book is full of it, too.

I. ENGLISH BOY

It's painful to be seen as a stereotype. Pinstripe suit, Windsor knot, shirt from Thomas Pink's shop, all as standardized and effacing as a military uniform. Smart? Yes. But the smartness is just proof you've got the self-discipline to do this job. We're an army. Like redcoats in their serried ranks assembled, you can spot us from a mile away: the tabloid hacks in training.

We're the New Cliché of Fleet Street. Look in the pubs down Canary Wharf. True, you can see a couple of the Old Clichés down there still, drinking themselves blind, collapsing, then rising again like Christ to write another article next day. But these days the pubs are occupied by an army. We march, we kill, we take no prisoners, we advance. And the lucky few advance *themselves*, become trusted advisers to the Supreme Commander, and sit at the Right Hand of Power Itself: columnists for Murdoch. Who has many hands, all of them on the right.

Well, if that's what you're thinking, then I've already thwarted your expectations. An unexpected advantage of the modern uniform, I reckon… camouflage.

Because I want to be a *Guardian* columnist.

Now it's true that all we ever think about, all *I* ever think about, is ambition. Advancement. Moving up to the heavies, we call it. Even the Editor here, I'm told, has a postcard on his desk—not that I've ever seen it—not that I've ever seen him—a postcard of a hippo, flying among the seagulls, with a caption: *Ambition Knows No Bounds*.

But I'm not so sure that's true. Because I never intended to be a journalist. Not in the least. From my days at Repton, possibly earlier, I'd longed for a career in pornography. But why drive mother into an early grave, I thought. So I settled for the most plausible alternative.

But there's no difference, really, is there? It's all about the shock of seeing what certain people manage to get up to in public. Or at least that's what I've begun to think. So allow me to provide an illustration. Because that's what journalism (or pornography) depends upon, no? Seeing the picture.

So. This was not long after 9/11.

9/11—when that doesn't get a giggle, I know I'm not at the office. But this *was* not long after 9/11, and I was meeting a friend of mine from Oxford, Lucy, an actress, barking shnarking mad but really quite lovely. One of those actresses who never quite *stops* acting. By which I mean, never stops making things up. I suspect she's got such outrageously sensitive social antennae that she can't let the truth get in the way of telling people what they want to hear. A skill I admire, given my line of work.

At any rate, Lucy had doublebooked me, so we were joined by the most appalling flock of Sloaney girls, really quite breathtakingly stupid, but fascinating to watch. So I just sat there and listened. It's the first skill you learn: not so much to make sure you don't miss anything (because gradually you realize nine-tenths of what anyone says is dross regardless) but more to keep them talking. You learn to project a sort of sympathetic, almost sexual, vacuity, which your quarry becomes more and more eager to fill up with verbiage. Until eventually they say something they hadn't meant to tell you, and you have a story.

Well, one of the Sloanes had been reading about the early years of Bin Laden. Before the woman-hating and the fascist death-squads, Osama was a swinging clubgoer in London. (Or she might have been thinking of Harry.) And now she's regaling us with what she read: '*Annabel's.* Do you *believe* it. I mean, *really. Imagine.* In the eighties, Osama Bin Laden was *there.* At *Annabel's.*'

Poor girl, it's clear she's never been to Annabel's, or she'd see how perfectly he'd blend in with the crowd there, even today. But she spoke with such melodramatic emphasis that I knew my Lucy would do something extreme. Because she's a lovely girl, but you must never, never upstage her.

Lucy speaks quietly. 'You know,' she says. 'I haven't told this to anyone.'

Meekly. So as to draw their interest in. You see why I love her, I've nicked most of my tactics from her.

And all the Sloanes lean forward.

'You see,' she whispers, 'I was a rather precocious fifteen-year-old. And I'd go to Annabel's. A friend of my sister's would take me. And he was—oh God—we had no idea who he was. Nobody did back then. But he was…persuasive. And one night, he bought me a pint of Bailey's. Can you imagine? A pint of Bailey's. I was fifteen, I drank it all—'

'And this was actually—' said one of the Sloanes.

'*Yes*,' she said, with real anguish. 'It was. He didn't have the beard then. Clean-shaven, with such—such *radiant* skin-tone for an international terrorist.'

'He's still got nice skin,' murmurs a Sloane.

Lucy continues: 'I was a girl, I was young—and after that pint of Bailey's, all I remember is that we were there, on the dance floor, and without even caring if anyone watched us, he…he *fingered me*.'

I couldn't have invented a better story. And considering I'm a journalist, it's not for lack of trying. But here's the punchline. A few days later I was having lunch with Lucy again. To congratulate her on that performance, actually. When her mobile rang.

He's even made stuff up

She picked it up. 'Hello? Yes, this is she. Yes. Yes. No.' (Her face went pale.) 'No, I have no comment about that, thank you, goodbye.'

I looked at her and realized: the unshockable Lucy Peacock was genuinely shocked. 'That,' she said, 'was the *Guardian*. Wanting to know if I had any comment on being fingerfucked by Bin Laden.'

And ladies and gentlemen, that is the quintessence of journalism.

Imagine *I'm* the man from the *Guardian*. Imagine me, mobile wedged 'twixt shoulder and ear, taking furious shorthand notes with my left, and pumping my cock with the right. And once I've got the full story, with climax—then I want you to imagine me *not* publishing it.

It's a world of hard work and cheap thrills It's highpaced

Because you must have suspected we don't tell you everything. We know all sorts of things that you don't.

12

Some of it's shoptalk: the reporter who killed his
wife, but the paper helped to have him declared
insane, so he's back at his desk and not in a prison.
Or the editor who's fucking Carol Vorderman,
perhaps to lay groundwork for some future insanity
defence. Or the well-known columnist who was
best known at Cambridge for sucking cock in the
King's College Chapel. And more general gossip:
which telly chef is a swinger, which Hollywood
homosexuals are closeted Scientologists, and who
fucked whom, and when, a week before Popbitch
tells you—the little people—so you can feel superior
for a day, the way that journalists do always.

Or important things, as well. Photos from Iraq.
You'll see them too—soon enough, I'm sure. And
once you do, I doubt you'll take issue with my claim
that journalism is pornography. No paper has run
those photos yet, but we've had a peek. And you
haven't. And that's the point.

I don't want to encourage paranoia. But really, do I
have any choice?

Because if I may talk, for a moment, about the
epistemology of smut—and you'll have to forgive me
using words like epistemology, like most professional
smutmongers, I read PPE at Oxford—but simply
put, it's in the nature of journalism to cause such
paranoia.

You want truth. You pick up the paper. But you don't
get truth. You get a story. And a story is built up
from facts, right? Solid English empirical facts, little
diamonds, hard as buggers, frequently overvalued,
and useless for anything save scratching up a
mirror—*unless.*

Unless a skilled professional strings them together, strings you along, by telling a story. And all a story requires is that, like children at bedtime, you believe.

And if you have doubts? Well then. You'll only end up wondering whether you can trust *anything* you read. Guessing at what might lie beneath the story, the spin. And by then, you're paranoid. Which, in some sense, is a perfectly reasonable response. I mean, far as I can tell, there's only one sensible reader of newspapers in Britain, and that's David Icke. Yes he peddles conspiracy theories about giant lizards pulling strings, yes he's loony, politically meaningless, no real power: since a paranoid is (God bless us) a thing of naught. But at least he knows that there's something *behind* what he reads.

Of course, poor David thinks that what's behind the newspaper stories is a cabal of extraterrestrial reptiles engaged in unspeakable sex orgies. Which is not a bad guess. Considering what's behind the stories is...*me.* An army of me. And we all know journalists love to flatter themselves that they *do* have cold blood and forked tongues.

But cut me out of *that* stereotype, please. I want to write for the *Guardian.*

II. AMERICAN GIRL

Prolly the first thing they teach you, growing up in West Virginia, is that our state is the marble capital of the world.

Not *marble* marble, like the stuff they make statues and stuff out of, like the, uh, Washington Monument or whatever. But marbles. The, uh, glass-beady

round things that kids are essposed to play with? I'm
not real sure how ya play. It's like, ya draw a circle
in the sand. And ya knock somebody else's out. And
if ya knock it out, ya keep it.

I *think* that's the rules, but it tells ya something that I
don't really know how to play. 'Cause the kids who
play good, play for keeps, they're competitive types.
They're goin places. They're gonna grow up, go to
college, and be rich. And we don't get that type in
West Virginia. Maybe ya get a glimpse a one, but
blink and the fucker's gone. Town I'm from's the
kinda place you drive through quick on your way to
someplace else. Pittsburgh thatta way, couple hours
drive in the other direction you find yourself in
Philadelphia, Baltimore—

Washington, DC.

And yeah, funny thing is, now they're talking
'bout me down there. Little old me. I can't think of
anybody else from West Virginia gets talked about
down there. I mean, yeah, we got some famous
people, like Loretta Lynn and—well, Loretta Lynn,
mainly. And, uh, Chuck Yeager. Guy broke the
sound barrier? Which like my momma useta say,
just tells ya how fast anybody with a brain wants to
get out.

Lord knows I did. So I did what ya do, signed up
and joined the army, spring of 2000. And for shit-
sure I wasn't counting on being sent anyplace. I
mean, not anyplace that's a theater of operations.
And least of all god-fucking-forsaken towelhead *Eye-
raq.* (No offense to any towelheads out there, that's
just what we call all y'all. I mean, better'n 'sand
nigger' anyhow.)

'Cause didn't we just *have* a war over there? I sorta remember that one, mean, I was a kid. And I know a lotta folks remember it from the, uh, cable television, CNN, but I had to tell 'em, where I'm from we can't afford no cable televisions. But I do remember some stuff, like the Bette Midler song, and I remember, like, seein tee-shirts of Saddam Hussein gettin fucked up the ass with a missile. You 'member that? It was like a cartoon, underneath it said, THIS SCUD'S FOR YOU. Heh.

But I don't know what that first war was *about*. To be honest, I don't even know what this war was about neither. But from my perspective, before you decide that I'm just pig-ignorant or somethin, I wanna ask you seriously: who *cares* what it's about? 'Cause with all the people on TV, wearin suits and sayin it's got something to do with 9/11, or *nothin* to do with 9/11, I just keep thinking: not like any a these guys is gonna get their ass shot off in Sadr City. And I don't blame 'em for that, but I do think it's worth mentioning.

And really I don't *have* to know what it's about, do I? For me it's a job. Kinda sucks, but most jobs do. And listen, if it sucks more to be a *girl* in the army, well fuck it, you try bein a girl in West Virginia. That *really* sucks. Like the drill useta say in basic training, he'd say: *YOU. WEST VIRGINIA. YOU A VIRGIN?* And I'd say: *SIR YES SIR.* And he'd say, *GUESS THAT MEANS YOU CAN RUN FASTER THAN YOUR BROTHER THEN, CANTCHA, SOLDIER.*

Cause that's the joke, see? How you define a virgin in West Virginia? It's a girl can run faster'n her brother. There's other jokes even worse'n that, but I won't tell 'em.

But my point is that yeah, I *can* run faster, faster'n my whole family, thank you very much. That's the plain truth of it, and I run straight into the arms a the army 'cause that's my way of running *out* of West Virginny. Only I didn't think it would get me so far away I'd end up where I did. Eye-raq.

Whole time I was there, Eye-raq, I kept thinkin about the night before I shipped out. 'Cause, y'know, they generally give ya a chance to spend it with your family—or sometimes they say your 'loved ones' in case you ain't got a family, but in my case let's call it a family. And they didn't, like, have a picnic for me or nothin. You'd think they'da give me a bar a striped ice cream with a little candle in it, or somethin, but no. They spent it like they'd spend any old fuckin Saturday night: six cases a PBR on the front porch an my father and brother goin through it like it's pink lemonade, and momma switchin off between cryin, and shouting at me for the things I ain't done yet she tole me to do before goin.

Then we look down off the porch and there's my granddaddy. He *wasn't* drinkin that night, which was kinda unusual, so we all lost track of him. But we see him there just—standin in the middle of the yard, lookin up at the moon over the far hills, and right then he just…I dunno, he *howled?* Not like a wolf or nothin, but… I'm thinkin, he's the only one a my family before me was in the service, and I'm thinkin: guess he don't envy me goin through whatever he went through in Korea. And now, he's just howlin at the fuckin moon.

But momma just says, 'Will you stop that GD racket, Daddy?' And he looks at all of us, embarrassed-like, and goes off for a walk in the woods. But he was the only one seemed bothered by me gettin sent off. Exceptin myself. My daddy, my brother, they couldn'ta give two shits. Even momma. She just said: 'Be sure to send some pictures home now, ya hear?'

Well, *shit.*

'Send some pictures home.'

Ya wonderin now if I made my momma proud?

I know I didn't. She came down an talk to me after the, uh, story gets loose, after I got sent back, sent here, and everything. And she just looks at me like—well I was gonna say lookin at me with stone-cold hate, but wasn't no different the way she looked at me most days, so I don't wanna make it sound special. And she just says: 'What the *fuck* you doin over there?'

And I just say, 'You know what it's like, momma. It was only foolin.' (Back then I think that's what I'm spose to say, so I say it: 'only foolin'.)

And she says: 'You think this is some kinda *game?*'

And I say: 'Yeah. I *know* it was some kinda game, momma, 'cause somebody somewhere drew a line in the sand and I didn't know nothin 'bout the rules. I just look down one morning and realize: *shit.* I have lost my marbles.'

Which, for those of you don't speak West Virginny, is another way of sayin: *howlin at the GD moon.*

III. ENGLISH BOY

Now I have to say that, in spite of what might seem my near-lecherous enthusiasm for it, what I do is a job like any other. I mean, it's rather dull sometimes. Much of the time.

The worst is Picture Captions. At this stage of the game, I can't escape doing them—someone's got to. But still, it's fucking dull. Example: magazine pre-releases a pic, hoping to boost sales for their next issue. They send it to us, our readers like a bit of vacuous totty—then I'm left to dream up a caption. *'You're-A-Vision! Pop contest hopeful Whatsername is set to represent the UK: here, she strips off for FHM.'*

You see what I've done there? It's a pun. 'You're-A-Vision'? Obviously that's crap, but it's the only way to amuse yourself—if not others—when you're the bastard writing the captions.

My difficulty is—well. I find myself staring at the photos and—and trying to work out what to say. Or why. Or how a tabloid newspaper can convey any meaning, as you leaf through and see it all, the tits and the footballers, the toddlers with cancer and the waitress who tells all about her kinky romp with the Chuckle Brothers—all of this beside a photo of—of something important. Something that's meant to mean something. But in this context, what possible context can you give it? With just a handful of words, printed under a photo of—

Listen. I'm not trying to sound wanky about it. I mean, I've made it sound like some sort of metaphysical dilemma but...but like I said, it's a job like any other, with rules. The most basic rule: there are two types of photos. The first is called the

Collect. Say someone's granny has been raped by a badger, you pop round to the family home and ask, 'Can we have a picture from the family album?' It's luck, but if you're the first on the scene, you can usually collect one. And the other type of photo is called, quite simply, the Snatch. That's when the paper's photographer takes the picture—regardless of whether or not the—

Well, see? What do I call the person being photographed? The *subject*, as though it were a portrait? Or the *victim*, as though it were a rape. Obviously rape is no laughing matter, certainly not if it's your granny, or your badger for that matter, but—

Well, here's a story. Some bloke had paid for his girlfriend to have a boob job, then she binned him and started working as an escort. Obviously this is news of genuine national interest, so they give it to me, because—well, because I'm good at this sort of job. Where you get the interview, then tell the story from an unsympathetic (if not hostile) point of view. Known in the trade as 'turning someone over'.

And this is not the first time I've turned someone over, as it were, but it *is* the first time I've turned over a woman. Still, stiff upper lip. Plus, she's an escort: I don't have to seduce, or *smile*, all I need to do is ring and make an appointment. We meet in a hotel room and I use what I would assume to be an appropriately charmless opener: 'My God. You've got *fantastic tits*.' But she's charmed.

We make small talk about the big tits, she doesn't mention they're fake—why would she, I'm not admitting I'm a journalist—but finally I gulp and I say: 'Listen. I think you're dead sexy, but I *do* have a wife and I'm not sure if I can go through with this.

I'll pay you for your time, just—not sure if the little soldier'd even salute. But—would you mind if I take a picture of your baps so I can have a shifty later whilst looking at them?'

And she's flattered and hey, less work for her, so she lifts her top and I snap the piccie. Then I suggest we leave together. Because we've got a photographer in the lobby, lying in wait for the second snatch. And I'd like us to be arm in arm when he snaps it, because that's all mother has ever wanted for me. To get my picture in the paper, I mean.

But in the lift there, Tits asks me: 'So, what do you *do*?'

Now the sticky thing is, there's something called the PCC—the Press Complaints Commission—which issues a code for journalists. And one of the big no-no's is: you're not supposed to misrepresent yourself. So I decide to be honest, but not 'cause that's *ethics*. Really I'm thinking: *it's worth a shot.* She might decide then and there to collaborate with us. Bigger story. Big as her tits. And I'd still turn her over when I write it up.

But I tell her I'm from a tabloid, and she went absolutely spare. By the time we get out of the lift, she's screaming rape, hotel calls the police, police show up—and the end result? She gets arrested for wasting police time. I go home unscathed, but they confiscate my fucking camera. No story. The job is ultimately, as one might expect, a complete bust. Tits went tits up.

But driving home, with her screams of rape still ringing in my ears, I'm thinking: 'This is the sort of work I have to do? If I want to move up to the heavies?' I was almost feeling like, like a bad person. What I did to her? Maybe it *was* rape. Or the moral equivalent.

Then I thought: No. That's just how she sees the world. And that's why she needs a–guardian. It's one thing to joke about being fingerfucked by Osama bin Laden. But it's something else altogether to understand that all of us—you or I or even Tits Herself—view the world through the lens of *power*. And an ordinary person's experience of power is invariably centred on its sexual manifestations. Which means: geopolitics, sexual politics, all the same. I'm not exaggerating. Whether it be Sexing Up a Dossier, or Invading a Fertile Crescent, or laying a Sustained Assault to the Sunni Triangle, and so on all the way up to the violent forced double-dicked detumescence of the Twin Towers… Yeah, sounds glib at first. Easy, vulgar, and therefore disgusting. But might it not also be accurate?

I wish I could thank that woman and her breasts for helping me reach this epiphany, though I doubt she'd understand. Still. You know I'm not jesting when I say my job, my *art*, is close to that of the pornographer. And if that disgusts you…well, you mustn't be disgusted with *me*. It's the way of the world, ducky. And while you are free to resent it, I'm not free to misrepresent it.

Unless I become a columnist. Then it's my job.

IV. AMERICAN GIRL

So we got shipped off to Eye-raq. And at first, it's not what I was expecting. 'Cause it's not a desert or nothin. There's actually a lotta green, and Baghdad? Well, shit, you'd be lucky to find a city like that in West Virginia. Say what you want about Saddam Hussein, he had real nice taste in architecture. I mean, not like he built it all himself or anything, but y'know, everything they did over there was to make him happy. So it musta been what he liked, y'know, lookin at all those palaces, lotsa pink pastel colors, like a petrified forest a girly birthday cakes, and stuff. I mean, I woulda been happy growin up there. 'Cept for the whole freedom thing.

Which is why we went over there, guess, but I don't think too much about *that*. 'Cause, uh, I gotta ask myself, I mean, if I'm an American and I got this *freedom*, well, what good is it? I mean, the Preznit's talkin 'bout it like it's so goddamn special, but I wish he'd just tell me what the bottom-line sticker-price cash-value is. Not to mention, why, if it's so special, if it's worth so much, why we're puttin our ass on the line to just—give it away. For free.

But yeah, it was a nice surprise to find out what Eye-raq was like. And it was the other kind a surprise when I find out what I'll be doing there. 'Cause me? They made a prison guard.

I guess I'm lucky I'm not directin traffic. That's what most of us was doing. But prison guard? God *damn*. Back at home, that's low. That's lower'n whale shit. Scum of the earth. Lookit. I had a cousin, name was Skeeter, which should tell ya something about what kinda PWT oxycontin-suckin lowlife *buttmunch* this guy was: Skeeter Dunkle. He worked at the state facility, and far as I could tell, his job was mainly helping people on the inside break the law *more*, takin twenny dollars here, twenny dollars there, arrange for them to get breaks, smugglin a bag a weed and what-all.

And he was kinda slow. And also kinda mean. And he wasn't real good looking neither: kinda guy they gotta tie a porkchop 'round his neck to get the dog to play with 'im. So I guess that's why one night, Skeeter goes over, and—'kay, there's this family up near where he lived, who are livin in a schoolbus? They don't drive it noplace, it's up on cinderblocks anyhow, they just live in it. I mean, it's got curtains and all. I can't remember the lady's name, but she's common-law married and they got a kid. These people almost made Skeeter look good. So one night he turns up 'round eleven, drags this lady outta the schoolbus and flashes some kinda phony badge, I guess corrections officers got a badge too, and he's got—I mean, can you believe what a dipshit this guy is?—he's got a *flare gun* pointed at her head, and gives her some fuckin story about how the schoolbus is parked illegally but he's gonna look the other way if she just, y'know, she puts his thing in her mouth. So she does.

But here's the point of the story, is, she tells the cops, and good ole Skeeter gets picked up, locked up, and shipped off to the same prison he useta guard. And the other guards? They know him. But they don't *wanna* know him. They just wanna feed him to the animals, American Gladiator style. And the animals in Skeeter's cage? They all know him too, but they ain't thinkin 'bout the times he did 'em favors.

They're thinkin about the times he used a billyclub. He's the enemy. So the first thing they done is they cut him with a shiv, straight across the belly, like *that*. So if he *does* get transferred to a different prison? Then all his new buddies gonna read that like a sign, and know what he is.

And what adds to Skeeter's problem is that he's a fuckin rapist. And far as they're concerned, well, that's the lowest of the low, 'cause you're pickin on women. And one night, he calls my daddy for his one phone call, and he's practically whispering, says: 'They got a rule in here, it's okay to rape a rapist.'

Well. I don't know if this is fortunate or unfortunate, but Skeeter didn't have to watch his ass in the shower too long. He was dead a week later. So many pieces that they couldn't even have a open casket at the funeral.

So that's my idea of what a prison guard's like. Not just Skeeter, but the other guards who're his buddies one day, and the next they're servin him up like chicken-fried steak to a pack a wild dogs.

'Cause it's like Charlie likes to say: Who Will Guard The Guardians Themselves.

Which I guess I should prolly tell ya about Charlie now, 'cause I'll be mentionin him, but. He was in charge a me. And I, uh. Look. Ya ain't supposed to do it but it happens. Fraternization. I mean, y'know, two people foolin around, or—or love. And I don't know if this was love, but—

Well, it's one of those things that just sweeps over you like, like a combine harvester munchin over the amber waves of grain. You get plucked, and shucked,

PETER MORRIS

and spun every which way till you don't even know
what you're doin anymore, or if it's *you* that's doin it.
I sure didn't.

And it's scary.

I know it's scary 'cause Charlie's kinda scary too.

Like, lemme tell ya. He come on real strong, and I
liked that, but it didn't—you know, it didn't *stop*. I
mean, I'm gonna tell ya this story but I don't want ya
to be shocked by it or nothin, but. We already done
the deed. I think it was our second time? I mean,
he was my first, ya prolly coulda guessed that, he
was my first but it was the second time we—y'know,
we done it—and I could kinda tell that there was
somethin, like, *behind* everything.

'Cause he's got that *thing*. Kinda like when you get
the Bible salesman turn up at your door, and he's
all smiles, but the minute you start talkin to him,
you can see the idea—pacin back an forth behind
his eyes, like a wolf in a zoo-cage—he's thinkin 'bout
how much he's gonna be able to screw ya for.

And it's worse if it's a Bible salesman 'cause he
thinks he's doin the Lord's Work. But the end result's
the same: wolf's gonna bite.

And that's what Charlie's like. When we were, uh,
makin love? I could tell there was somethin else
behind it, somethin that wasn't too pretty, somethin
like: *how far can I make this bitch go.*

Which he coulda just asked me! 'Cause the answer,
frankly, was, far as you wanna go, mister man! You
ain't gonna shock me.

But we're not sayin any of this. This is just what's behind our eyes.

So we're layin there and what he *does* say, he says, 'Tell me, kid, would you do anything for your babydaddy and for the US Army in which he serves?'

And I just look at him, and I say, 'You know I would.'

And he just says: 'Good.' And then he, uh—

He hauls off an punches me right here.

She indicates her breast.

And oh I screamed and I cried, and I'm thinkin, oh God I shoulda known *this* is what I'd end up with, momma tole me, but— He ended up calming me down, 'cause that's what he's good at. Bible salesman. Charlie can talk his way out of a GD sunburn, lemme tell ya. But the thing that stuck with me is—

Is what I saw in his eyes. Right after he did that. 'Cause, uh.

'Cause I didn't see *nothing*. There was *nothing* in his eyes right after. Like hittin me was what it took to make the big bad wolf lay down and have hisself a nap.

Then later he says: 'Maybe we should get another girl to join the fun.'

And I'm like: 'Whaddya think this is, Charlie, fuckin *France*?'

And he says: 'This is Eye-raq, kid. And whatever you wanna say about this godforsaken outhouse, we know there's no French people here.' Then he says: 'Y'ever hear of a harem? It's what they do in this part of the world. Maybe we should give it a try.'

And I said: 'Charlie, there's plentya shit they do in this part of the world, and the reason we're here is 'cause we're *not* gonna give it a try. Isn't that so?'

And he doesn't say nothing. But I see something start movin back behind his eyes again, and I'm wonderin what it's gonna take the next time, for the wolf to go to sleep.

V. ENGLISH BOY

Wednesday night. Working late, in the attempt to get noticed. Instead I get completely fucked over, the one job worse than Picture Captions—the Weather Roundup. As I'm staring at reports of more rain in East Anglia, Lucy calls, I tell her I can't meet for a drink because I've got to write *this*. And she says: 'Can't you just make it up?'

No. That's why it's so fucking dull. It's there, we discuss it, we complain about it, but nobody can do anything. There's no *spin* can you put on weather. What can you do? Not much, except lie back and enjoy it. Seldom possible, even in Blair's Britain.

But when I leave the offices, demoralised, I look at my watch, and—it's Wednesday, so I think—

Well, look. I can admit to you, I can admit it: I do, in my spare time, enjoy the occasional visit to an S&M club. (Not as a card-carrying member:

more of a fellow traveller.) What else can I say? An Englishman fixates on his schooldays particularly when he went to the sort of second-tier public school I did: think Christopher Hitchens. Then think The Torture Garden. The Hoist in Vauxhall, The Backstreet in Mile End. Or, there's a military night at Substation South in Brixton. 'Boot Camp.' Ever been? Wednesday nights. Like going to Hell as a tourist.

And I suppose you're free to find it sordid or baffling, something you can't *empathise* with. Although if you were better able to empathise, you might share my interest in S&M. Because they're the same thing. You can't actually feel another person's pain. What a ghastly phrase that is: 'I feel your pain.' Whenever anyone says that, I feel like responding, 'Can't you feel my *cock* instead?' I mean, if you want to enjoy yourself by sharing some pain with me, why don't we just have rough sex, I'll slap you around, maybe throttle you a bit. Wouldn't that be better than all this soulful moist-eyed Blairism?

So: taxi to Brixton, just across from the tube, and down a rather grim-looking industrial flight of stairs into a basement, where the scene is fascist: no fats or fems. Where the aides-de-camp are AIDS and Camp. Where haunted-looking men in military fatigues, or even the occasional Luftwaffe uniform, wander off into the warren of dark alleys behind the dance floor. What's back there? A dark cubicle with a fisting-sling? The HIVIP Room? I don't know, I don't follow them that far. I'm not one of them, one of the Damned, with those dull eyes like they've lost their taste for life but soldier on in search of more pain, marching onward to the Lowest Circle of Gay Hell.

I'm exaggerating a bit, but really, this *is* Gay Hell, and it's *not* my scene. (I prefer Heaven.)

But then I notice: some of the Damned have formed an orderly queue. I go to look. And I see him. The boot-polishing boy.

The club hires him: polish your boots for three quid. You can even wank while he does it, although he'll warn you, with surprising steeliness, that if you get one drop of spunk on him, it'll cost you twenty extra. A bit younger than me, shirtless, with one of those little military caps, you know—

> *He puts thumb against thumb, index finger against index finger. He holds the shape horizontally, like an eye.*

Dark hair, dark eyes, olive skin…so smooth you want to leave *marks*. Portuguese maybe? Or perhaps some fairground Gyppo *mélange adultère de tout,* the perfect downtrodden boot-boy. In any case…he's my type.

After the queue's been polished off, I offer to buy him a drink. Assuming, rightly, he'll be glad to see someone his own age, who's not one of the Damned. We talk. As it turns out, he's been hired not only because he's fit enough to attract the punters, but also because he has a, well, semi-professional interest in all this…

He's in the TA.

My journalistic curiosity—among other things—is aroused. Frankly, I'd only ever thought of the TA as a sort of ghastly joke, Gareth on *The Office*. But he's telling me that he loves it. 'It's like stress relief.'

Goes in for the weekly drill, the monthly weekend, the two weeks per year of fulltime camp, and—this is what he says: 'You don't *think*. Don't think about work, paying the rent, *anything*. You just do what you're told.'

And I'm fascinated. Astonished. Delighted to discover an urban homosexual who can restrict himself to just two weeks per year of fulltime camp. But more than that: he's given me all the clues. Wears a uniform. Prefers *not* to think. Does what he's told. And in this club, for Christ's sake? He's a *submissive*. It's a match. So I don't bother to angle and wrangle. I just announce, coolly, we're going to his. (I'd take him to mine, but it's a long way to Belsize Park, and mother might hear.) But in no time, we're in his flat, near Peckham, or somewhere, not sure, south of the river is all Lewisham to me—

And he shuts the door behind us, moves towards me, maybe for a snog, and I look right in his eyes, and slap him across the face.

He moans. With pleasure, I think. But one never knows for sure.

Now I won't go into too much detail here, lest I frighten the horses. But I need to tell you about the important bit. He's naked, face down, I'm spanking him, *hard*, because it's painful being an English stereotype. And I'm calling him all sorts of names, as one does, with a sort of military flavour to the whole thing really: *you worthless fucking cunt, the army will teach you to fucking obey me.* Et cetera. And then, to enlist him in his own humiliation, I ask him for suggestions: *What are you?* And he says, y'know: I'm a cunt, pussy, bitch, all the obvious, but then—

He says: '*STAB*. I'm a STAB.'

I maintain my character, 'cause it's a scene. (It's *my* scene.) But I have to ask: 'What's that mean?'

And he says: 'It means Sad TA Bastard. *Sir.*'

Well, under it all, I'm a journalist, I want the story, so I ask him: 'Who calls you that, boy?'

And he says; 'The regular army men. *Sir.*'

'Like me?' I say.

He whimpers in the affirmative, so I say: 'Tell me what else to call you.'

And he says: 'Call me TWAT.'

And I'm thinking: Call you a twat? I call that rather feeble. So I pick up my belt from the bed, and aim for the balls. A hit. He screams: '*Stands for Trains Weekends And Tuesdays. Sir!*'

My God, more vocabulary, like a French lesson *avec* the Marquis de Sade: French *With* Tears. And I know there's got to be more. So I say, with a deadly evenness of tone: 'What do you call *me.*'

Automatic: 'I call you Sir. Sir.'

'No. What do you call me behind my back.'

He pauses then: 'ARAB, Sir.'

The other end of the belt now, catch his limp bell-end with the buckle, and he positively writhes. I say: 'Arab. Why. You think about killing me?'

(There is a war on, after all. And who knows, a boy like this might listen to The Cure.)

But he says: 'No, Sir. Stands for Arrogant Regular Army Bastard, Sir. Sorry, Sir.'

Isn't that amazing? I had no idea. So I dropped the belt because there's only one place left to go from here. And you can imagine that bit, because frankly fucking is fucking and...and this was *transcendent.* I wanted to live in that moment. Wanted the experience to linger. I mean, I already knew I'd see him again—this was too good a match—but more than that: I wanted something to hold onto. A souvenir. With most encounters like this, the best you can hope to take home with you is non-specific urethritis. But here I am thinking: what if I could—

Take a photograph.

That's all. But I felt like I *understood* something right then. That life is uncertain, it's frightening—and moments in time, even the perfect ones, never stop and linger. They get discarded, like yesterday's newspaper, unless you make some—*monument* to the moment. Some spectacular image. So I understand. Always bring a camera to avoid the pain of disappointment.

And God I know this must sound like frightful nonsense, but what can I say? I'm in love.

VI. AMERICAN GIRL

So I told you all about Charlie, you must be thinkin gosh, now we got an explanation for the shit went down. Her man was mean to her, boo-hoo. Like everytime there's a lady on the TV shoots her husband or sets fire to his bed, cuts off his tallywhacker with a steak-knife, y'all say: Well hey, he beat her up, course she's gonna snap.

But I say: sometimes when a woman shoots her man, she just does it 'cause she's a bitch. Or a *badass*. And I say, sometimes when a woman gets beat, she deserves it.

So the thing you gotta understand 'bout what went down, is…I mean, at first…well, it was kinda… interesting.

And the interesting thing about interesting is: it don't mean fun, and it don't mean good, necessarily. It means interesting. And when you're in the army doing a shit job overseas and you got those—idle hands? Well. You start to think *interesting*'s better'n the opposite.

It's how I was thinking about…'bout Charlie. Before him, nobody ever did sex to me. So's not like I really had anything to compare him with. Although one of the other girls who worked the prison with us, Abby, everybody called her Abs or Sixpack—I don't even know why I was talking to her, I mean, she's probably like eighty percent Lesbo anyway, but when you're out in the middle a fuckin nowhere you gotta talk to *somebody*—so I'm talkin to Abs, who, if you need a mental picture to look at while I'm sayin this, well, she's what my daddy would call a carpenter's dream: flat as a board and never been screwed.

So I don't know why I'm turning to her for sex advice, 'cause—well, anybody knows less'n me, it's *her*—but I'm sayin: 'Abs, is it normal for a girl, y'know, is it normal to get, uh, bruises on your titties from sex?'

And y'know, I *knew* it wasn't normal. That's why I'm tellin Abby that, maybe you won't believe it but it's the God's honest truth: I was bragging.

But she says: 'God, no, that's not normal—honey, you all right? Did somebody *do* something?'

Like she's my *grammaw* and I come home after the junior prom with my dress ripped, stinkin of splashed SoCo and my eyes all pink from cryin. But that's not what happened. So I say to her: 'Nah. That's not what happened.'

And then I grin an say: 'I guess I know now, I wasn't doin it right—but least I know that, Jesus H Christ, doin it wrong sure is fun.'

But that's the part that gets me. 'Cause it was. It was a lot like fun. I mean, the bad kinda fun. The *badass* kind. And, uh, the thing is—

Well, at first, it's like, Charlie's doin what he wants to me. And I take it all 'cause, well, 'cause it's sexy to do that. You gotta know that: it was sexy. When somebody's on top a you hammering away, it gives you a reason to be there: take a lickin, keep on tickin. Harder they hit ya, the faster ya bounce back up. Like one a those inflatable clown punching bags.

'Cause I took shit all my life, and now, *now,* I'm finally getting a chance to show somebody what I'm made of. Prove I can take it, prove I'm strong. Like I'm sayin to this big dumb man—'cause he is dumb, he thinks he's smart but he's really dumb—I'm sayin: c'mon and see what I'm made of. 'Cause you ain't gonna split me in half no matter how hard ya come.

And I know what men are thinking when they roll off ya. They're thinking, 'Shit. Lookit her lyin there.

When I'm done, I just wipe myself off, pull up my pants, and walk away. Army man shoots, cleans his rifle, reloads for the next target. But what's it like for *her*? She ain't gonna walk away, she's lyin there half-broke. And I *know*. I just *know*. She's still gonna feel me hittin her deep inside, long after I forgot her name.'

But girls know better. It ain't like that.

'Cause I know that's why they get rough, why Charlie got—

They wanna fuck you, so you stay fucked.

But that's the great thing about bein a girl. You can just keep on taking it. I mean, you prolly gotta freshen things up with a little Mazola so's you don't get rug-burn up in there, but that's the point. They think they're stronger 'cause they hit ya. But they just don't know what it means to be *so* strong you can lie there and take it.

That was all I thought. When Charlie kept, y'know, pushing it that extra little bit further. But the turning point for me—and look, this is gonna sound silly.

Charlie tells me: 'Come on over to my room tonight, bitch.' (And I know what you must be thinking, he called me bitch, but it wasn't like that, it was just a game he had goin.) But when I get there, he's got—the porn. He's not lookin at it, he's playin a Playstation or somethin, shootin at a TV since they won't let him do it in the streets. But there it is, with somethin for every taste, as much as you'd ever need, all spread out like the Old Country Buffet a porn.

And that was one thing that I had, like, no experience with, or anything, is the porn. 'Cause he managed to get quite a collection going, lemme tell ya. Which is funny to think that we're there in some part a the world where they think a girl showin her ankles off is slutty—and here's Charlie with, like, the world's most biggest collection of skin mags. And not just, y'know, *Playboy*-type tittymags. He's got stuff that goes, like, places you didn't even know any person ever wanted to go. You just can't believe anybody would make this, let alone buy it. *Farm Fuck? Schindler's Fist?*

And I'm not shocked. I don't go in for shock. But Charlie, he wants me to be turned on by it. So I gotta pretend. (Charlie's a man—he can't tell the difference.) But all I'm thinkin is: *these women buy toothpaste.* Isn't that crazy? That's what's goin through my mind. *These women buy toothpaste, just like anybody.*

And then it hits me, the reason I'm thinking that. It's 'cause they're all smiling. And that's what's creepy. 'Cause it looks fake and you can only fake a smile so far.

And it's not like I'm thinking the stuff they're doing is so dirty they must be miserable. By now, I done most a that stuff, not all, but still. I'm happy as a clam. The problem is they're *pictures.* And that means there was *someone else there,* holdin a camera. And you know what girls are like. Which is: they're normal one-on-one but with other people watchin 'em, they get mighty different. 'Cause, two people in a room, two girls, you can level with each other. More than that, you got a party, you got a audience, you start *acting.* You start *lying.*

And what scares me most is that the girls in the magazine are pretendin to smile, I'm pretendin to be turned on by them—but Charlie's dick ain't pretendin. And what scares me is: Charlie's a man. He can't tell the difference. So what're ya sposed to do?

You're sposed to start *lyin*. You start *acting*. Like, above and beyond whoever's watching you. Till you're just smilin and shakin your ass like you're Julia Roberts and who's watching is *the world*.

Which, considering what Charlie got us into next… now it is.

VII. ENGLISH BOY

I took this job anticipating the *thrill*. Where you write, someone else subs the story to fit the space, someone else, some creative genius, designs the page or sets the type, someone drives the lorries and takes it off to twelve million readers. And there it is. The first draft of history.

And for the first time, I'm part of it.

Now I had a Scottish political editor who used to refer to writing your story as 'baking a cake'. Meaning that, like a chef, you need someone to give you the initial ingredient. A suggestion. And then, you can cook up the rest yourself.

So. It's the boyf who suggested things.

But first I'll say. Now that the photos from Abu Ghraib are published, we can see and agree: it's an atrocity. But when I first had a peek, like a shameful glance at dirty postcards in a drawer—

Look. You know enough about my private life to understand this. When I first saw those photos, it occurred to me—in spite of that American girl with the kicked-looking face: a munter like that puts any man, gay *or* straight, off his stroke—but seeing the photos, it struck me that all this might be, well—fun to try. I mean, even that girl is grinning. Now, principle dictates that you only do such things in the privacy of your own dungeon, and only with an Iraqi insurgent with whom you have enjoyed a longstanding monogamous relationship, but...I was fascinated.

And more's the point, after many dull nights writing Picture Captions, I thought: who's going to write the captions for these? What can you say? What words wouldn't seem superfluous or bathetic beside images like this? They achieve the quality, quite nearly, of beggaring description altogether. They're practically art.

And yet...

And yet the biggest difficulty I had with those images was trying to work out what they *mean.* If we're seeing them at all, surely the American government has some reason for showing them? I know that sounds outrageous, sounds like a loony conspiracy theory of David Icke's reptilian proportions, but—it does cross your mind. Because otherwise, it's a cock-up of such magnitude that one suspects not even the Americans could have perpetrated it.

Or worse than paranoia, it might simply be that it makes no difference. Pictures like these won't stop America, no more than a glimpse of the Dying Gaul could have stopped Caesar.

But what if they'd been photos of *British* soldiers?
I mean, given the strength and numbers already
of the anti-war movement here, mightn't that do
something? If nothing else, it would underscore the
masochistic devotion of our government to their
masters in Washington. And it could do a great deal
more…

I was thinking about all this at the boyf's place. We'd
just had a sesh, we're both exhausted and I'd pulled
a muscle in my arm, I'm lying on the bed reading
something lighthearted by Antonio Negri. Boyf's
at the computer. Then I realize I need a pencil to
annotate, so I get up, and instinctively he moves to
cover the computer screen.

Well, if this is love—and who's to say it isn't—then
it means never having to say I'm sorry. So I grab
his wrist, yank it away, and look at the screen. And
realize. He's chatting on Gaydar. With ten or twelve
different blokes. Clearly the TA has taught him to
multitask.

So I bend his wrist back till he cries out, and move
in for a closer look, to see their photos. It's Gaydar
but a few do have photos of their faces. Dull-eyed,
haunted-looking, passports from Gay Hell…my boyf
is trading instant messages with the Damned.

So I start to read and—I don't read all. Just…enough.
Enough to understand the scenes they describe are
beyond my filthiest ambitions. They make Pasolini's
Salò seem vanilla.

But it appears the boyf's been trying arrange a scene.
Later that night, on the Heath. (How he'd get there
from Peckham is beyond me: I suppose he'd walk,

he's a masochist.) A scene where all of these men would—use him at once.

So I take a breath. And think.

I think: Fucking hell, if he weren't queer and begging for this, you'd call it queer-bashing. What *is* he? I think: He's an addict, a sex addict, but I can handle that, how many alcoholics have I handled on Fleet Street? Same thing, only you're *swilling* at both ends—

And I think: So. If he's a slave to his own darkest desires—I might as well make him a slave to mine. Because—

Because I love him.

And he prefers bondage to love. Or believes that love is bondage. So. To love him, I must *own* him. Look down at this filthy slave, and say—Shakespeare, right?—*this thing of darkness I acknowledge mine.*

So I say it.

I mean, I don't say *that,* cause he's fucking thick, he wouldn't know Shakespeare if the Bard kicked him in the cunt. What I say, I pull him up by the twisted wrist, look him in the eye, and say: 'No. You can *not* do this. Because—'

He looks in my eyes for a sign of weakness. He doesn't see it. I take a breath, and continue.

'Because I own you. You *cunt.* You belong to me. And if you need something more than what I dole out? Then *beg* me. And if I'm nice I'll make it happen. Give you what you need, or what you deserve.'

So he tells me. Long, detailed, brutal. Less like sex, more like—Guernica.

And I say: 'All right.'

And then, almost without thinking, I say: 'Just one thing.'

I say: 'I'm bringing a camera.'

And he's so excited, he *hugs* me. 'Round the knees.

So I start to make it happen, but I'm *careful.* The boyf may be indiscriminate, but I've got a bigger plan by now, the scene is part of a larger drama, it must be perfectly cast. I require discretion above all else. We find two regular army men, just back from Iraq. The rest I recruit from Boot Camp: some muscle-queens who seem quite fit. And seem fit to wear the Queen's Uniform.

And of course the boyf could supply us with rifles: part of his fantasy's to get bashed with an A-1. And since we're sneaking into the barracks for this, I order him to arrange a truck, a four-tonner, for set-dressing.

And the anticipation made him beautiful. I've told you he's my type. I've told you he looks almost Portuguese. But that evening he looked—

Like an Iraqi insurgent with whom I enjoy a longstanding monogamous relationship.

I won't describe it.

The pictures are worth more than any number of words. They're worth quite a bit in pounds sterling too, as it happens.

But there's one thing I must describe. It was just a
moment. As I pulled my leg back to kick him, and
realized that—that I was actually drooling. So wholly
possessed I couldn't even keep my mouth shut. The
last thing I remember, really. Is me, slackjawed,
slavering, slipping away into—some other world.
Like a spastic, a paedophile, some subhuman
creature charging forward, fully in the grip of its own
mindless concupiscence. An American.

Everything after was a blur. Really, in my memory, it
only exists as—

As a series of snapshots.

The rest was a piece of piss. Hand off the snaps to
the soldiers, bring them round the offices, a quick
word with my superiors… Paper's cautious at first.
I'm told the Editor is hesitant: says we caught
a circulation cold over this whole war business.
Opposing the war made us look unpatriotic.

Then the photos from Abu Ghraib are finally
published. And suddenly, it's all a very different
story.

Of course I'm not assigned to write it. That goes to
someone important. But they're running the story,
it's out tomorrow. And tonight—he spoke to me. The
Editor. He didn't seem to know my name, but came
up to thank me, in person.

'You know what this'll be like?' he said. 'That
Vietnamese girl, running naked, burned by napalm.'

And what pops into my mind is General
Westmoreland, who claimed the picture was fake,
the girl merely burnt by a hibachi. But all I say is:

'I'm proud the paper is leading with this story. I'd heard you were hesitating.'

And he said: 'I was. But now—fuck 'em. If they don't like it, well. You're clever, I reckon you know what the Duke of Wellington said, don't you? Don't recall who he said it to, but you know what he said.'

And I said: 'You mean: *Publish and Be Damned.*'

And the Editor roared with laughter and put his arm round my shoulder. Although I couldn't resist adding, like Jeeves to his feckless master: 'I think you'll find it was Harriette Wilson to whom he said it. *Sir.*'

And now. Come round to see the boyf, he let me in, then fell asleep straight away. He's been sleeping *very* soundly since that night. Me, I'm wide awake. Adrenalin. Anticipation. Because—

Because tomorrow, for the first time, my picture is going to be in the paper. Not that I can tell mother.

VIII. AMERICAN GIRL

Well, and now's the part of the story that everybody knows already, which makes me kinda not wanna tell it. You wonder if any a these newspapers met me, they'd actually think that somehow this was my big idea or what. 'Cause I mean, whatever else I might be, I'm a girl. And *girl* means—

Look, I don't know why it took the world so long to let girls into the army. 'Cause frankly, we been learning the game since the time we were kids, whereas the boys don't.

Women understand a chain of command. How the army works.

Bein a woman, you know from the outset that sometimes you are expected to shut up and take it. Either you are gonna be the one makes the coffee? Or else, if you're lucky, you get to sit there, listen, take notes like a secretary. And then some girl brings *you* a cup a coffee, and you look at her, thinkin: ha ha, least that's one day where I'm not the one's gotta take it like a bitch and make the coffee.

I don't actually drink coffee myself, but you understand what I'm saying.

Whereas boys think it's all up for grabs. So when you got two boys fightin, they gonna wrestle until one of 'em sticks his dick in the other. And they don't always do it obvious-like: but when they screw each other *up* or *over,* it's still screwin, ain't it? And that's what happened with the Preznit and Saddam Hussein, and we know who wound up getting assfucked on that particular occasion. But when you're a girl? Well. Fat chance you're gonna be the one sticks your dick in the other guy, 'cause by and large, you ain't *got* a dick.

So we know who's gonna wind up gettin assfucked on this occasion too. And what more can I say, 'cept: ya know why some boys like to assfuck their girlfriends all the time? I'll tell ya. 'Cause it's the only thing they worry some bigger boy's gonna do to them.

But listen. About how the army works? 'Kay, I joined up 'cause my career goal was: *get the hell outta the Appalachian*s. But ya gotta have a certain kinda state of mind to get outta the town you grew up in, join the service and learn some kinda skill. You gotta have a *open* mind. And most a the army's like that. Nobody's gonna look at you funny if you make friends with a black fella who's workin 'longside you. That's a requirement. That's the army: if you can't play on a team like that, a team that's basically like a perfect slice of America, well then. There's an awful lot at stake. There's America at stake. So you all play by the rules, and you learn to *like* the folks you're in the army with. 'Cause they're America too. Like my daddy would shit hisself if he saw me with colored friends, but my job's to form a *unit* here. And if that's an American soldier next to you, don't matter what color he is: he's your buddy, you watch his back.

Which also means, if you got prejudices, you save it up and you only let loose when you got the enemy in your crosshairs. 'Cause that sumbitch—well, whatever you wanna say about him, he's...he's not America.

So that's the way it was with Charlie. He's my buddy. He's watchin my back. And if I got any dissatisfactions with 'im, well, like it or not he's America.

But here I am in a big fuckin city—I reckon Baghdad's even bigger than DC, or maybe it just looks it—and they don't even speak English here, and I sure as shit don't know where I'm goin, so—what else can I do? I just—y'know, took a safety-pin, and took my own little piece a confidence—cause I only got a little piece, not much—and I go to Charlie. And I pin what I got to the end a the tail a his big fucking red-white-and-blue kite. And up it goes, up into the sky.

Bur when that kite-string snaps and it's all floatin off into the fuckin pure blue *nothing*... Well. There's a piece a me went with it. And it's like that's where I was. Eight miles high an lookin down at myself. And people are lookin back up at you too, so ya better smile an look purty.

But what am I thinking up there? That I can't even believe what I'm seein. What I'm doin. But I just know: even if I yelled out, top a my lungs, yelled out *that ain't right*, who's gonna hear me from way up there?

And I'm not really way up there. I'm down below.

Down all the way under the prison buildings, some dark cubicle, some interrogation area, with Charlie standin guard. With a broke-off mop handle in his fist. And this time, I can read it, the look in his eyes says: *You do not question me. You got problems with what I'm tellin you to do? Then may I suggest you do what I'm gonna do. You take those problems, and you take 'em out, take 'em all out on this brown person's ass, the ass that's sittin on the floor in front a you, smeared with its own shit, dogs barkin at it—and in fact? I think this brown person's talkin out his ass now, screaming and cryin and beggin his Fictional Fuckin God to do something about the sitchyation, and save that ass. Well. I don't know what he can do, girl. But I know what you can do...*

So it falls on me. And I guess now I'm gettin blamed for not makin the right decision. Whatever that woulda been.

'Cause what I got is a job to do. And my job is to do it.

And even if some—some person's sittin on the floor
there cryin, comes a point where it's your ass or his,
and all you can think when you look at—at him is:
who the fuck is this person and why should I care?

Oh, but *you* care. Well, lemme tell y'all: it's easier
to care if you ain't there hearin it. It's easier
when you're sittin comfy at home in that fuckin
Barcalounger, feet up watchin cable TV, never at
risk a bein blowed up in a car bomb, gettin shot.
By enemies, by friendly fire, or gettin shot by the
shots the gummint gives ya, protect against chemical
warfare and leave ya fucked for good. You're never
at risk a havin your body flyed back from half a
world away, in a Ziploc fuckin freezer baggie, take-
me-home-country-road.

Which means it's easier for you to care about that
dumb Eye-raqi sumbitch than it is to care about me
an my fellow soldiers. 'Cause what we do, what I do,
what I get *made* to do, makes y'all feel guilty. Makes
ya feel bad.

Not just what we do in Eye-raq. I'm talking 'bout
the whole US Army here. What we do all across the
GD planet, just for you. Air Force takes the sky and
the Navy takes the water. The Corps got the Halls
a Montezuma and the Shores a Tripoli covered,
which sounds like a easy job to me, no matter what
they want ya to believe. But the US Army? We go
everyplace else. Which means: anywhere on the
globe where shit gets spilled, and they need a girl
with a mop. To mop shit up. Before it oozes on down
to the bottom of your easy chair. You know that.
And that's why you feel bad.

But how I see it? Me and that brown person on the floor, we're the same, almost. We both had a run a bad luck. Was he in the wrong place at the wrong time? Maybe he don't have no useful information? Well. Tough Titty, Miss Kitty. He's still in jail, we still gonna hate him, just 'cause he happened to be in Baghdad that particular day. Like me.

But when I get shipped back here, everybody's sayin: that, uh, even if there *were* orders from above—which we got no evidence that there was, *of course*—it is no defense to say she was just following orders.

And what can I say back to that? 'Cept: hey dumbass, listen up. I'm *in* the army, I work 'longside these people, I am one a them, and trust me: they're good people but they ain't smart enough to organize a peanut-butter-and-jelly sandwich. I love 'em but man, these people could fuck up a baked potato. And now, Senator, you want 'em making decisions about, about—what's Right and what's Wrong?

Which, I might note, is not a rule those boys lay down on themselves. Fuck up when you're me, they sell you down the river, baby. But fuck up when you're the Preznit? Two weeks later and who remembers?

So. Here I am now, down the river. And what'm I gonna do about it?

Sit here and cry?

You know: I *could* do that. But I tole ya. I know this better'n most. Cryin for y'all's a great way to make you start thinking: Who the fuck is this person and why should I care?

IX. ENGLISH BOY

And another news cycle has come and gone, and the scandal is forgotten. Deciduous, discarded. Although you may perhaps have noted, I've moved on to the heavies. Got my own column, got my own place, north of the river, and moved the boyf in with me. Timmy. Timmy's his name, I need to remind myself to use it, he's not a pot-plant.

So yeah. I'm a rockstar. In which case: why am I so fucking depressed?

It's not guilt. They couldn't trace the photos back to me, the squaddies kept their mouths shut, as did the boyf, who's nothing if not obedient. No chance I'd be implicated.

But when they saw through the hoax—the wrong hats, the wrong bootlaces for fuck's sake—when the pictures backfired, I had to start supplying words. Spin. So I came forward, revealed a few things—I mean, they taught me how to turn someone over, it was simple enough to turn over the Editor. Suggesting he'd not seen through this forgery because it fit too perfectly with his own leftist anti-war agenda. But then…I had to attack the agenda. Which wasn't difficult. Even the best marksman is partial to a spot of sitting duck on occasion.

And it all worked. I'm a columnist. Although not, needless to say, for the *Guardian.*

But I don't care. I understand now: I don't have principles like that. Nor does the *Guardian.* End of the day, what's our job? From Weather Roundup to Influential Columnist, we pretend we're providing an important public service: speak truth to power,

face the unpleasant facts, enlighten our readers…
Bullshit, really.

Imagine I'm a surgeon. You'd think of me one way
if I said I went into private practice to make loads of
cash. And you'd have an altogether different opinion
if I said I worked for the National Health, because I
thought that it was vitally important to help people.

But what might you think of me if I told you that
really, I took the job because I enjoy dispassionately
thrusting sharp metal objects into living flesh?
Because that is what surgeons do. They just seldom
emphasize it that way.

So. It's not about principles. The sad truth is: this
job is—just a job. To thrust the metal deeper into the
flesh. I don't speak truth to power. If anything, I'm
speaking power to truth. Those are facts and any
further spin I put on them, is just—pretending.

But let's pretend for a moment. That I did it because
I had principles, left-wing principles. So I tried to
do something idealistic that resulted in a shambolic
mess. (Like many leftists.) And let's call what I did
'framing the guilty'. I looked at the war, I called it
criminal, and I fabricated evidence to stop it. It's the
same way the war got started, after all. Framing the
guilty's what Britain and America did to Saddam
Hussein.

Good story, no? Unfortunately: not the truth.
Otherwise I'd be at the *Guardian.*

So let's pretend again. I had right-wing principles,
and wanted to discredit the anti-war protesters. All
those sheep, bleating over and over again, 'Not in
Our Name.' Because let's face it, they are tedious,

aren't they? Fucking dull. So let's say I peddled a transparent fraud, because I liked the idea of bringing the pacifists into disrepute, making their side seem as duplicitous as the government's.

Well, if that's what I did, it's sheer genius, by virtue of its total arse-backward implausibility. But no. Again, it's just a story, not the truth.

The truth is: I wanted to be a columnist. Now I am.

Why?

Power.

And Power has no principles. And Power can't be counterfeited. That's why my photos were revealed as fakes. Put mine next to Abu Ghraib. Put Britain next to America. Britain's got principles, of course. We're reminded whenever we see Blair, perched like Jiminy Cricket on the shoulder of the Pinocchio President. But British photos couldn't pass for real atrocities any more than Blair could pass for a Texas cowboy. And the difference is Power. Behind Abu Ghraib is the might of an empire. And those photos are a monument to conquest, to torture-worship—like Trajan's Column, a pure and unmistakable exercise of Power without responsibilities, Power for its own sake.

And at the end of the day, you must have some respect for that. And for me. Since I've got a bit of power myself: I'm an Influential Columnist now, at least until the novelty of a pro-war homosexual has worn off. But my column's not like Trajan's Column: it's more subtle, I think, more like a Fifth Column. But I'm on fifty grand a year, and best of all, they're taking freelance pieces from me at *Attitude*.

But the bewildering part is—

It's strange to feel this, but more and more—

I've lost my taste for it.

There's no joy. Lucy avoids me, she says I've
changed. And she's right. More and more I feel like
one of those *old* hacks on Fleet Street. Rise at six
and write until I feel the thirst overwhelm me, for a
poison I can't get in the pubs down Canary Wharf.
More and more I feel like one of the Damned. Lost
the taste but I soldier on in search of—more and
more.

So the boyf and I—Timmy—go out at night. The
Hoist, The Backstreet, Wednesdays to Boot Camp.
And we go all the way back, behind the dance floor,
to the darkest cubicles. And I can't tell you what
happens. I can't tell you what they do to him, as he
hangs there like a pot-plant in a sling.

I can tell you that he takes what they give him.
Because ambition knows no bounds. Even if one's
ambition is simply, like Christ's, to suffer. So he takes
it. Like a man.

And I can tell you what I do.

I stand there, with my eyes fixed on his. Unblinking.
Like a reptile. And I watch his face, as these men do
what men do. Like I'm watching a show. Like I'm
looking at a photo. And I try to understand that this
is *real.* I can't feel his pain. But I can at least believe
in it.

Then we stagger home at dawn. And say we love
each other.

We say it often. We love each other. We say it much as politicians say they love their country. Not to convince the public, as is often supposed. More to convince themselves.

Because if we didn't call it love, what would we call it?

We'd call it a man's game. Call it *war*. And the pleasure of war is pain. Our sexual conquests are military conquests, and all-male death squad: the Army of the Damned. Hating women, and life, and ourselves.

But we can't say *that*, ducky. I told you before: stereotypes are painful, and I am, after all, a *Gay Man*. Although this has nothing to do with being gay. It's all about being a *man*.

So isn't it nicer to say we love each other? Because men so seldom do that. Then we fall asleep together. Then I'm up at six, alone, to write.

But I don't enjoy it. Look at the photo next to my column tomorrow. Right there, in black and white. You'll notice. My eyes look…dull.

Because really, politics is just the Weather Roundup, all over again. Or else it's like being raped. There's plenty to complain about, but not much to *do*. Except tell the nice people to lie back and enjoy it.

X. AMERICAN GIRL

It takes a lot for somebody like me to become famous, lemme tell ya. It's like lightning striking or something. Crazy weather. But it's not good-famous. It's like Saddam-Hussein-famous. All 'cause I did my job. Followed the chain a command.

And my job was kinda like hot dogs. You kin only enjoy 'em long as you don't see what goes into 'em. If they took pictures at the factory, dumpin in a big barrel full a pig lips and assholes to make that wiener, you'd go get yerself an apple instead.

'Cause look. Everybody in the world seen me doing what I did wrong. Which—here's the funny part—it only proves that really, I'm nobody. 'Cause the powerful people? The folks I was takin orders from? They're invisible.

But try it now. Do what I did. Follow that chain a command. All the way up to the Preznit. 'Cause ya know, I almost feel bad for the Preznit a little. I think he's a fuckin disgrace, but I feel a little bad. 'Cause ya look at him and ya know he's like me. He's in over his head, no fuckin clue, but there he is—still smilin for the cameras.

And ya look at him smilin, the poor dumb bastard. Like Howdy Doody. 'Cause he's a GD marionette. He's takin orders from above. Just like me.

And you can't *see* where that chain goes up to from the Preznit. But trust me, even the Preznit gets his marchin orders from someplace. Somebody, some*thing*, is pullin his strings. Something invisible, all-powerful, something that's got the whole world in its hands. Ya know what I'm talking about, right?

Not God, dumbass: I'm talkin 'bout *money*. I know the Preznit *thinks* his orders come from God, but trust me, I seen what George Bush was doin to Eye-raq and it was not the Lord's Work.

But the Power a Money's *like* the Power a God. You can't see it. You can't win if you fight it. And when it's on your side, it can make you the Preznit, baby. Long as you do what it tells ya. Even if it tells ya: go to war.

And those guys are like God 'cause you can blame 'em for all the shit that happens—you *should* blame 'em, 'cause it's their fault—but you can't catch 'em and haul *their* ass into a court-martial like you're doin with me. Know why?

'Cause you don't got pictures a them. They're invisible.

'Cause they're the ones *behind* the camera.

Makin a movie, makin the porn. Givin all a you somethin to look at, distract you, while they leave the scene of the crime.

So that's why you all seen those pictures of me. To give you something new to hate. And it works. Now Charlie hates me. My momma hates me. My whole family, everybody I ever known. Ain't even comin to the trial.

But fuckit. I don't wanna sound like, y'know, ohh let's have a pity-party for me. 'Cause actually, the only one who counts'll be there. My granddaddy.

He comes to visit, coupla times a week, and when he turns up, he wears his ole Korean War uniform—y'know, with the medals and all right across here, and he's wearin his cunt-cap: I hate to use that word, but that's what they call 'em, y'know, the kind that looks like *this*—

> *She puts thumb against thumb, index finger against index finger, and holds the shape vertically, like a cunt.*

And when he just come in like that, they all salute him. My, uh, prison guards. Same ones walk me back to my cell after, and they call me really mean things. But hey, it's the brig, I don't expect polite.

But Granddaddy, he just sits there, totally silent. He's always been a quiet fella, prolly never said more than a hundred words to me my whole life. I think that's what he musta learned as a infantryman: ya don't need to say nothin if you got patience. So I'm learnin that from him now.

And someday I'll be an old soldier like him. And you can look in my eyes and then you'll understand it, all a you. You'll understand.

How I been screwed.

How I ain't never even seen the faces of the men that screwed me.

Although I kin be pretty sure they're men.

And you'll understand how that is what men do.

And maybe I'm just thinking about this 'cause—I'm gonna have a baby now. Sucks, right? You only got one person ever did the sex to ya, and most a the time he's stickin it places that you ain't gonna get a baby unless God Hisself miracles one down on ya—and somehow, I draw the short straw. Lightning striking again. But like I said: some men wanna fuck you so you stay fucked. And that's called having a baby.

They'll take it away from me, though. Give it to my momma, and if I'm not allowed to see that baby, then I'll tell her: 'Be sure and send some pictures to me, y'hear?'

And when I'm alone in bed at night, and I'm thinking about all the things I ain't got? Like my baby. Or a family. Or *freedom*—good ole American freedoms like I was helping unload on Eye-raq.

Well, even though I ain't got any a those things, there's one thing that I can hold onto. Which is this: *I served.* I served my country, now I'm servin time for a mistake. And someday, all y'all are gonna say: Hey, hold on a minute, she only got into all that shit 'cause of a whole nother bigger mistake. But nobody ever went to prison for *that* one. And that ain't fair. That ain't right.

And when that day comes, y'all gonna see me as a hero.

So maybe I can remind you to keep lookin for those other guys. The perpetrators. 'Cause in case you didn't notice? While you was out at the movies, or busy jerkin off to the Internets, or looking at pictures of me on television, I gotta tell you. Somebody broke into your country and stole it. Sorry, ma'am. Sorry, sir.

But it's not too late to do something about it. Like the Preznit useta say: hunt 'em down, smoke 'em out. Maybe you can find 'em someday. Just remember—they ain't the ones *in* the pictures.

And till ya find 'em? Just wave goodbye to me. As I get marched off to prison. Smiling. Smiling as I go.

Like I was smiling in all those pictures ya saw. Like all the women are always smiling in the skin mags. Like girls everywhere learn to fake a smile. 'Cause boys can't tell the difference.

But hey. We all buy toothpaste, right?

So smile, y'all.

Smile.

End of Play.

Acknowledgements

I'd like to thank the following for their assistance: Marian, Muffy, and Joseph; Mary Hinz; John Buzzetti and Nick Harris; Liz Gately and Nico Muhly; Adam Thirlwell; Andrew Chippindale; Katy Brand; and all those I interviewed for firsthand accounts of life on Fleet Street and in West Virginia, or service in the British Territorial Army, the US Army, and the Iraq War. I'd also like to thank the following for suggestions: Mark Ravenhill (with whom I had dinner on the day the Abu Ghraib story broke); Colleen Werthmann (who told me to write this play); and of course the ever-suggestive Katherine Parkinson. Finally I must acknowledge Johann Hari (or 'Mata Hari' as I call her) who continues to suggest so many things, to me and to all of us, some of which pop up in these pages–only the merest soupçon, I'm sure, of what pops up in the course of a heavy session with Johann and colleagues like Christopher Hitchens or Andrew Sullivan.

WWW.OBERONBOOKS.COM